Watching the Perseids

poems

Jed Myers

Sacramento Poetry Center Press

Published by Sacramento Poetry Center Press
1719 25th Street
Sacramento, CA 95816

cover design and art: Rosanne Olson
back cover photo by Roseanne Olson
book design by Tim Kahl

Typeset in Garamond

ISBN-13: 978-0-9831362-9-3

Acknowledgments

I am grateful to the editors and staff of the journals noted below in which the following poems in this collection originally appeared:

Atlanta Review: "My Grandfather's Tomatoes"
Broad River Review: "Sure of What's Needed"
California Quarterly: "Same Fire"
Crab Creek Review: "The Ghost in His Chest"
Drash: "Study in Red"
Euphony: "Loyal"
Garfield Lake Review: "Blue"
Heron Tree: "This One Leaf"
I-70 Review: "Wingtip Shoes"
Journal of the American Medical Association: "The Atoms in the Cancer," "Buy New Floss," "Who He Is"
Minetta Review: "A Strut to Set"
Naugatuck River Review: "Brain Tumor with Stardust"
Prairie Schooner: "Innocence"
Schuylkill Valley Journal: "Selfish Wishes"
The Summerset Review: "Leveled"
Talking River: "Weeds"
Wild Violet: "Before It Disappeared," "No Conversation"

"My Grandfather's Tomatoes" also appeared in *The Meridian Anthology of Contemporary Poetry*

"Same Fire" also appeared in *Generations of Poetry* and *Two Countries: Daughters and Sons of Immigrant Parents*

"Loyal" also appeared in *Floating Bridge Review*

My thanks go to many, more than I can name in this space, who have fostered the creation of this book. The encouragements of fellow poets T. Clear, Jim Bertolino, Kathleen Flenniken, Ted McMahon, Peter Munro, and C. Albert have been especially valuable. Charlene Breedlove, who edits poetry for *JAMA*, has blessed me with her incisive eye and ear. My son Jonas Myers has given this collection many hours of close editorial review, and his guidance has been invaluable. Bob Stanley and Tim Kahl of Sacramento Poetry Center have graciously made the actual book possible. And Rosanne Olson has lovingly created the cover imagery within which these pages now rest. To all these dear allies and many others, I am deeply grateful.

Table of Contents

One — Until

Two — Since

Watching the Perseids

for my mother and brother,
who also loved him

One

Until

Cruising Home

I'm lying right on the bed beside him.
He keeps catching his breath
from the trek up out of the kitchen.

We're talking memory drifts—
time that rented Sunfish
capsized in the river, summer

evenings playing catch before dinner,
the night *his* father died....
This winter day, bright

outside, from here behind
the white curtains no one opens—
a soft haze of the lost

possibilities. He couldn't say
if it's October or March—it's neither.
But this his last February is

itself a river of what
we, together, happen
to remember. He clears his throat,

windpipe boggy already
since he's reclined—he tells me,
in that gravelly stutter,

his feelings have gotten too strong.
Oh, he knows they've been there,
inside his chest all along,

since he was the young man he was,
cruising home from work in the Buick,
becoming and becoming my father—

now it's harder. Up through the neck
and against his face from behind,
pressing out through the eyes, contorting

his lips—he gurgles, sputters,
I haven't done enough for you yet.
And fueled by a few gasps,

just as when they lowered his father,
he can't help it, he cries.
Then it's over. He continues to forget.

Leveled

The pocket of chaos in my father's head,
so far, has left him unable
to walk, find words, lift food on a fork,
or know what day it is. It makes him
emotional—he weeps as I enter
the room in which he reclines for hours
a day on his hospital bed. He speaks
with a new stutter, says *Help me*
whenever he comes to a hole in the ground
of his memory. *Yes, it was*
Connie Mack Stadium, Dad—I knew
what he was getting at. I see it too,
as it was, out past Strawberry Mansion
in the summer evening light. It was leveled
decades ago, when he never wept.

Selfish Wishes

There are some hard parts to watching him die.
I'm thinking of one—I hate

to admit it—we'll never have met
on the shore of Lake Como. Well he didn't

promise. Knew he'd be busy
eyeing and handling those silk prints

on into evening. What about dinner?
I'd ask. He wouldn't answer.

I wanted to be there once, hear him order
Caprese in the musical tongue of his host.

I wanted more. I'm ashamed
to come clean. Take the train to Rome,

perhaps find the oldest synagogue
together, just look at it still standing—

we might not even enter.
But work. It came first.

He wanted to have put plenty away
for us, for our kids, for a time

like this. Here we are. No more trips.
Thank you for listening to this one

hard part—my selfish wishes.
I have to add how I wanted

to hear him play that old clarinet—
he led a swing band with it in high school!

I had the thing fixed, but he wouldn't
pick it up for a minute, even

when he was well. I didn't get it.
But he sings the old hits more and more

as his brain's taken over by tumor.
He laughs and weeps easily now.

I'll have to let his bed and my chair
beside it be where we meet on the shore

of that distant water. Perhaps
we'll share some cheese and tomato, and find it

delicious as it is there. We'll enter
the oldest temple in time, or at least

I'll see him off at the door. I'll listen
for a fine reed in the silence.

The Atoms in the Cancer

On the left side of my father's brain,
in the core of the glioblastoma,
the cells reproduce so fast
they crowd, press, get crushed like grapes,
and create a pool, a necrotic gemisch,

in which, yet, every atom remains
pristine—electrons in faithful orbit,
nucleons tireless in their quantum
vibrancy, mesons ecstatic
in their quiverings—just like each atom

in the intricate neuron lattice
on the right side that lets Dad think
What's this trouble saying November?
Every atom equally happy,
none in the least impaired,

whether it lives in the chaotic nation
of new decay or in the elegant
strands of the opposite hemisphere.
These tiny immortal pirates! They
dance in and out of reckless alliances—

we are their shipwrecks. They couldn't
care—they'd be glad in the jaws
of ants on a monument-studded hillside.
Our atoms, I imagine, will shimmer
as joyfully in the void between planets

as in the murderous density of Earth's
core. The atoms in the cancer
liquefying once-conscious terrain

on the left side of my father's brain—
they'd be thrilled to join in composing

mushroom spores drawing moisture
from the ground in the shade of an oak
on that slope overlooking the river, or
to take part in the blackness of crows'
feathers flapping in the oak's limbs.

And those atoms won't mind being torn
to plasma in the hearts of stars.

Same Fire

I lost my name half a century before
I was born. Across the Atlantic
a ship came, bearded man on the deck,
same fire in his chest as mine,
preparing himself to give up
whatever can be forsaken, shaved,
stripped, or hidden away nameless
in his nervous marrow, to save
that spinning flame (he doesn't know
it's there behind his awareness, the harbor
too bright with churn and wake, tugs
and heaving crowds, too loud
with horses, groaning docks, men
unlashing crates—too much crashing
at his senses, for him to sense
the roar under his breath, the engine
that drives him to this shore). He stands
and waits to answer the cold uniform
questions that will pour through the grating
in the clearinghouse down the ramp,
where he will further unknow himself,
his tongue will fail his grandfather
glaring at him through the east wall,
his curls will splash out from under
the black wool hat, he'll forget
to mouth the familiar blessing
for this moment of his arrival
in the new wilderness. He's willing
to lay down the white silk of his ritual
fringes on the concrete, to walk over it
if this is his pathway to the street.
He's already sold his prayer book
at a dark shop in Leeds—he's told himself

as if in prayer, over and over,
he comes from nowhere, and practiced
the melodics of all the accents
flooding his ears. The deafening
crash and clang, stomp-march of boots
and carts, hooves, horn-blasts, gears,
government stamps pounding the blotters,
the howls, cheers, and chatter
of the ten thousand tramps
awaiting official passage into chaos
and all its chances, *is* the music
to which he chants (devout
as the sons of Aaron who disappear
into fire) out into the empty
basin of his processor's face,
his new name, by which he will go
where the fire takes him.

Here I am
Great-Grandfather, one burning
branch of your profane devotion.

Weeds

Alone on the lawn outside
our corner brick row house,
I gathered dandelions for my mother.

She would know my love
by this, the flowers
like suns, like the sun in my chest

beaming thanks for her being
and mine. I tore the stems
from the source in those stars of leaves,

held the blazes in my fist
and ran, up the steps
and in, across the gold carpet

to the kitchen, where she turned
her eyes on my gift. She placed them
in a jar on the sill, and let me know

as she did so, with a smile,
I should know they are weeds.
They glowed in the window-light, blind to their nature.

Still in the Crib

Still in the shade of the café umbrella
on that Paris promenade, being offered
a cigarette by the young fella from Spain
whose English is charming, I'm waiting,
my wife in the shop of ten thousand French buttons.

Still asleep on that Whidbey Island
beach, my head on the thigh of a girl
whose back's propped on a log—she watches
a man and his son fish the surf
for the ocean-bright coho marauding through
to fight their way to their births and die.

And still on call—the old woman
whose ribs I've cracked to keep her alive
dreams her husband drives by
in his '59 T-Bird. She wants to climb
in with him for another long ride.

I'm still dreaming I'm something
like 29, not even married
yet, and she can't help but want me
where her mind doesn't legislate, body
its own country, still free tonight.

Too young to show you my age
on upraised fingers, I still fly
the storm clouds of desire and fury
my mother can't see. She scowls
at herself, not me—I can't tell. She cries
for her mother. The formula's ready.

Still speeding on my red Schwinn
down Sorrento Road to the quiet hiss
of the wide tires, that long
dangerous kiss my only contact
with my home planet, its black macadam
waiting to skin my palms in the crash.

I'm still in the nest—the night,
my apartment, my bed, this body
a bony dream tent, the dream itself,
these layers of comfort for the loss
of the comfort of not being yet.

Every instant still occupied—it
is as it ever was. The atoms,
the light, the space, never forget.

Dad still thin, agile, tan
as the clay courts he plays tennis on
every summer Sunday—no tumor
behind his left temple, no forgetting
his curled right hand, no trouble
pronouncing *Jefferson Hospital.*

Still at the breast. The original
emptiness wakes up and sings for something
something like a hundred and seventeen times
a minute. The cry upon hatching
never gives. I'm still in the crib
this earth denizenship is, thrashing.

Brain Tumor with Stardust

He recalls the old songs even better now.
Taps the one hand he still thinks is his
on the bedspread, beams at the unseen
audience, sings like he's got the whole band
behind him—he was never like this.

Back before seatbelts, nights on the road
home from the drive-in show in the black
Buick, Mom beside him up front,
I'd be slumped in the back half-asleep

and hear him—*Sometimes*
I wonder why I spend
the lonely nights
dreaming of a song…,

stirred by just a word of conversation
between them. She'd join in…
they'd bicker a little over the lyrics.
Yes, that much—then quiet again.

Now, the teenaged bandleader unhinged,
he swings the one arm he owns in the air
out over the bed, conducting *"A" Train*
into the room, a packed high school gym,
sweat-humid, pheromone-tinged!

The headboard and lampshades disappear
in the dim kept in by the curtains, and young
dancers composed of dust motes spin, swing-
step to the tempo of his air baton, then

he takes up his transparent clarinet
and sputters a throaty frenetic solo—
a burble of blue-white surf, thrash
of a breaker rolling toward us, ghost-
father and ghost-son standing
together on the Atlantic City shore...

I can hear the cymbal-crash, and the theme....

Lord, the abandoned hand's uncurled,
first time in weeks, its fingers working
the silver keys. My eyes are blurred
with sea. He's the happy maniac,
last wisps of what suddenly-white hair
the rads have spared brushed wide by a gust
off the beach...ah, we are everywhere

we've been together—yes, and before,
in the ballrooms, on the roads, by the waters
and in the halls of his era, I'm there
with him now! A breath, a breath...he tires.
His eyelids lower, the gimp hand falls back
into that closed repose of neglect,

limp at his side, in the room
where he snores—a brushed snare
or a janitor's broom. The dancers have died.

Buy New Floss

Remember, tomorrow: Trim nails,
shred sales slips, shower,
call that lawyer who tells it
like it is, restring your guitar.
Better not wait on the bills.
When you shop, think fiber.

The letter you wrote your daughter
last week, left on the seat
in your car—mail it. Take an hour
walk after dinner. Regard
the moon and Jupiter, should they appear,
and even if not, while you're looking,
take a breath and forget who you are.

If that proves difficult, go
have a bourbon with a splash of water
at the alehouse. Take a seat
at the bar and meditate—stare
at the graying man in the mirror,
if it hasn't gotten too late.

You do need your sleep to work
the list. Get to the barber,
call your mother again
while her carotids are still open,
talk to your father as long
as he'll stay on the phone, forget
the tumor taking his brain over.

The following evening, maybe
Jupiter will grant you a breath
of its pure anonymity. It requires

no report of you. You're not
on its list. Renew your passport.
Vacuum. Buy new floss
while your molars are still yours.
The moon is a terrible dentist.

My Grandfather's Tomatoes

I still see them, round and shining, red,
pale green, and all the nameless shades between,
still smell that back-of-throat itch from the leaves,
and feel the heft of shears in my small hand
while he loops twine around the stakes and stems.
He'd hoist me up to pick the ripest, then
we'd run it to the kitchen, find the knife,
and slice through skin and seedy flesh—the sweet
and acid meat would lie wet on rye bread.
We'd have our feast. He'd smile, boyish-like,
to watch me eat, and like me, wipe his lips
with wrist and back of hand. Now I'm as old
as he was then. But when I hold one ripe
tomato in my grasp, he smiles again.

Who He Is

Ballooned on Decadron, cheeks shined
under sugar-water eyes, he cries
soon as we trundle into his bedroom
to say our goodbyes. He can't find his
glasses—they've wandered again.
The steroid's filled in his wrinkles
with that sudden smooth fat. He smiles,
wet face like a moon, like a mutated
child's, nearly hairless cartoon
of the eighty-three-year-old man he is.

He still is who he is—tumor presses
his brain against the wall of his skull,
and will, and will—for how many weeks?—
till the swell of the cells, who he is
and isn't together, squeezes through
the hole in the bony enclosure's floor.
That'll stop breathing for sure. He won't be
who he is anymore. So the evening
dose of the slower of all swelling is
raised, two milligrams to four. So?

Let his bones crumble, his immunity
lose its edge against the *staph aureus*
occupying his hot red elbow—
let his emotions swirl in the hormonal
whirlwind, inhibition's lids torn
loose in the chemical blow. Let all
his blood sugars go, limbs grow spindly
and limp. Let his forgetful hand drop
the cup every time he tries to wrap
his dry lips around *Hello.* Let Decadron

take of him what it will, so long
as it lets him be who he is, who is now
stuttering into the vision of Murray's
Delicatessen for lunch. He wants
to climb out of bed, drive if he could.
His thinned-out eyebrows rise, those
of a kid with an appetite taking in
the shine of a succulent world, giving us
his wishfulness, looking ahead
at the time of his life, every bit who he is.

Wayne

I heard them say it—*Wayne,*
the place he drove in the black
Buick before we woke, not back
till we were tucked away again. What

was it? Where he went to work.
Sold houses—that's how they put it.
I knew Wayne as the name of his being
gone. We roamed the neighborhood

till dark, tossed a ball till we couldn't
see it, then it came to Whispering
Down the Lane, leaning on cars,
hoods still warm from other fathers'

cruises home. Ours, the handsomest
and best-dressed dad in this row-house
universe—the finest the last
to pull in. And he must have earned us

the most, those hours at such
mysterious distance, at the end
of a pristine turnpike they'd made for men
like him. Like the men we wanted

to become, in houses that stand
alone, their own greens around them,
under a sun burning away
the sticky humidity we shuffled in

on the asphalt expanse of our summer
games, our purposeless fun.
Wayne, the shining land our god
Dad came from, visiting

Mom for the night, each night.
Now he's dying. I still dream
of Wayne—I find a crossroads,
a few stone walls surrounding

a square, a fountain—something
like the tiny village he drove us to
one summer in Québec. I don't find him
there. Don't know why I've come.

Where the Truth Goes

Our off-white woolly terrier took it
all. Eyes like pools in atolls,
like telescope oculars, tunnels

lit with remote repose, he gathered
our secret seethings. Wildness honed
to witness, he was my first

analyst, no axe of his own
neurosis to grind. Even my mother's
need to watch while he ate, it seemed,

he didn't mind—he collected
all of the data, integrating it
into a tacit equation for what

mammals want. A wonder, how much
he noticed—how Dad would enter
a cinema scene with each cigarette,

my brother's stutter like trips
over love's invisible fracture lines,
my interior disappearances

behind screens of the best behavior—
down to my mother's insistence
we give up the dog, as we would

for the move to the house with tracks
and a creek, as she was convinced
he'd get himself crushed or drowned.

He watched all this, till he was driven
off in the lady's back seat—off
to watch somewhere else, who knows

how many of our heartwritten notes
hidden under his ivory fleece.
So much goes unreported.

His Next Success

No more chemo. Doc's called it,
thinks it's a month or two at best.
Dad can't get it. That part
of his cortex that could've—it's shot.

He's upstairs in his bed all day—
assisted to the kitchen for dinner
dressed in sweats or a robe
thrown over his underwear. But he's sure

he'll get back out there. He'll drive
the Jaguar down to 30th Street
Station, catch the *Acela Express*
to Manhattan.... It'll be soon,

a morning in March. Is it a blessing
he's missing the synapses he'd need
to be bitter or afraid? No matter
if Mom *klopfs* him over his *kopf* with it—

if God sends a bold-print letter
embossed in gold, an invitation
to resettle his soul in Heaven,
no old bones to lug down the hall—

he won't get it. In weeks
he'll be mumbling marble-eyed in that winter
light that sifts through the sheer
curtains they keep closed all day.

I'll see his face in that light—
luminous as he begins to forget
to draw breath. He'll never have thought

This is it. He'll cruise, weightless,

across what for him is no precipice.
Whenever he brought us, it did seem
effortless, how he'd hail the taxi
in seconds, in the mad crush and wail

outside the station, surfaced again
in his chosen metropolis, on the way
to his next towering success, close
as he'll ever imagine himself to Heaven.

The Vigilant Ones

Dad knew me as he knew himself—
we stood before the world's mirror
and held still for the old tailor
Italo crouched to pin our cuffs.

Through that window the gone world droned
our history—we were visible
to those left restless in the shtetl.
They looked and looked at us,
a century crossed in the silver glass.

They oohed and whistled, proud of us
and mocking at once—that silk,
that wool, that smooth lapel....
We who'd come loose, we dwelled
as gentlemen among the gentiles, dressed
like Merion Cricket Club members in good
standing—Dad glad for the ancestors
watching him hand the navy blazer
back to Italo then slide his arms
into the silk-lined camel's hair jacket
in need of an alteration, I

muttering in my chest to the dead
in their beet garden, I'm sorry, sad
it's come to disguises as Dad insists
my worsted three-button's vent is spread
by my ass, can't his old friend
with pins in his lips let out the seam
at the waist? Go ahead, mark it—
his son's got to look like a mensch.

That audience both cheers and kvetches,
even now, behind every mirror,
though Dad and Italo lie
in their cancer beds. It persists,
just as I witnessed when I was six
at Brooks Brothers in Manhattan. I had to
wear the best. I hated it then—
those devoted ghosts sneering
as I modeled heavy herringbone coats
that would never make sense to my friends.

But I also saw those shimmering
torn men smile and nod in their tatters—
they'd have done no better than Dad
on this side of the glass in the name
of Melech ha'Olam.

In my bathroom
mirror, a face bearing ancient features—
its lips close and part. I hear myself
pray, to no great Observer who calls
my soul through the ceiling and walls. I whisper
to the vigilant ones who stand a few feet
behind my shoulders. They worry
the fringes of their worn silk shawls,
praying for me, to live, to eat.

No Conversation

Knowing that he was soon to die, I
dreamt of Heaven, a wide deck
suspended over a highway. I was
checking it out as a care facility—
the chairs and chaise lounges rickety
things, woven plastic straps
lashed to aluminum tubing.

There were areas out of the glare,
under corrugated green fiberglass
awnings up on wrought-iron struts.
And the dead all about were milling
in variable states of haze,
in tennis outfits, bathing suits.
Where were the courts, the pools?

No conversation—only the drone
of the road below. Nothing new
to learn from that real-world song. I left
for the parking garage. Could I tell
my father about this place? Would I
want him to know, or just let him
see for himself when it's time?

Serene

My son heard my father say it,
no one else there in the bedroom,
in that dim-lit quiet, and my son,
a man already, had to lean in,
bring his ear closer to those dry lips
to be sure, my father's voice
so soft not just for the lack
of adequate breath—he was telling
a kind of secret. The old man had
risen early and driven himself
late into the night, slept poorly,
given his weekends to errands
and chores—the tailor, the laundry,
picking up everything on the list
my mother would hand him, the bills
to be paid, the stonemason's
storm repair on the creek wall
to be overseen.... I remember
my father all my years attending
to needs. He'd fly to meet my mother
for a few days of her month-long winter
vacation in Florida—phone to his ear
back in the room through the afternoon,
making things work. So the secret
he vouchsafed to my son, and
that my son could not keep, it was
in a way blasphemous for my father
to say—that death might be
beautiful and *serene*. Oh,
I'd heard my father say beautiful
often—beautiful job,
beautiful stadium, jacket, tie,
beautiful kindhearted guy. But

never *serene*. I'd remember.
That was not a word in the world
where he lived and worked. It would be
serene soon—no need to rise
and see to the working of things. I think
he spoke to my son, as an asking
permission, requesting leave,
asking the one he felt most willing
to grant it. The one most like him.
The one who would take care of things.

Innocence

Memory's the thing. The fish
hooked on the end of that string, hoisted
high, a live iridescent
disc, perplexed eye on each side—
it hung like a lone wind chime....

My grandfather hollered like the kid
I knew he was, *You*
caught that sunfish! But he lied—
he was the one who'd lifted that life
to the sky, out of the public pond

on the map of my memory, that day
in Fairmount Park. I was five,
the air far brighter than older
eyes could admit, the crowd of waders
a sparkling carnival of spirits

come to shine incarnate
in the earthly light. But memory,
kind servant, might
protect me here—maybe
it was I hauled the sunfish out,

dragged it onto the sand
and dirt among the soda cans,
cigarette ends, and tossed
wrappers. Did I poke it
with a stick? Was I six?

Was the fish ours? Perhaps
an older kid beside us,
who'd learned to pierce the worm

with his hook, had let us look.
All I'm sure of's this—

I saw a thoughtless dying
radiant thing—it hung,
gasped, turned in the stir
of useless air, in the wind of light
and time. It still hangs there.

A Strut to Set

The story had a twisted power, Adam's
rib the source of Eve. My mother,
sitting on my bed before our goodnight
kiss, read to me the ancient stories
she herself did not believe. I knew—
she sighed and looked away between the lies—
it seemed she trusted no man's love, no loft

inside where she was crushed, her father lost
to dust before she'd grown. So I dreamed
a rib out of my chest, a strut
to set behind her breast against the threat
of breath's collapse. I'd heard those gasps
and sobs, and seen her taken, once,
on someone's arm, to that place they'd called

the hospital, and I'd inhaled some sense
of death. I wondered, without thought,
would my small slat of bone preserve the life
my life depended on? It was such magic,
not God alone, that gathered up the dust
to make a wife for Adam. That stick
beneath my skin, along the edge of abdomen—

could it keep her crumpled soul propped open?
I snapped it loose somehow, inserted it—
we lived! But at the site of my extraction,
even now, a reef of wound weeps violet
blooms of doubt on every woman's skin,
stain that can't be taken out once in,
the seepage of my own love's disbelief.

Blessing Between Us

Now he's gone primal
creature, broken
the lifelong treaty
he's kept with reason.

He's flailing, even
against the Liberian
aide who can't lift him
back onto the bed

from the floor, the bleed
in the heart of the tumor
crowding the thought-light
out of his head.

Mom can't handle it—
we'll have to ship him
off to a soft-lit
place made for dying.

I'll change my flight—
red-eye arriving
next Friday morning.
Maybe I'll make it

in time for a sedative-
dimmed glimmer
of blessing between us,
a kind of good night.

In the Grip

A dog will delight in your trust
when you let it bite your hand
with enough of that sharp tooth
press, that impassioned jaw's
grip, to hold you there,

no tension in your wrist
or arm, the knowing between you,
your skin will not be torn,
your flesh come to no harm.
It's an assurance of your bond.

Yesterday, my father,
exhausted again from the last
round of his blind alarm,
crashing back into half-awareness
he's in hospice, can't leave

for the next train, for the restaurant
meeting he'd arranged in the recent
history of his delirium, lifted
my hand to his mouth and bit down,
long and firm, on a knuckle.

No IVs in Hospice

If we get more water into him
he could liven up, enough
perhaps to enjoy our visit.

No IVs in Hospice. He sips
the Diet Coke he loves from a straw
we place between parched lips.

But his thirst is almost lost.
Hunger's gone. He hurries,
lying there in his pale blue gown,

off to a meeting. He's got to
get on that train. Why is everyone
standing around like there's nothing

left to accomplish? Getting water
into him could just swell
the madness. No IVs in Hospice.

Two weeks ago the tumor bled.
Rushed to the ER, he got fluid
through a tube, came to,

and on the phone with me, he said,
Don't worry—almost lucid.
Then he was brought to this place—

strange, quiet, meant for comfort
while dying. No IVs
in Hospice. He accepts

another sip, while he peers
through the white ceiling, watching
for the train he must not miss,

water of life low in his veins...

More Comfortable

Over-drugged on Haldol, under-
hydrated with a saline trickle,
kept manageable by such
measures—too weak to grab
the rail, to tear his gown off
one more time. Too hard
to just unlid his eyes. No
trouble now. Can't get through
the sentence *Let's get out of here*
tonight. I know they think
they're keeping him, not themselves,
more comfortable. Still,
he tries to speak—breath
a raspy gurgle, can't clear
his throat, can hardly sip
the least few drops of Diet Coke—
keeps starting with *I never....*
Never what? My ear
right at his lips...no matter.
I never...thought you'd be here?
Dad, I'd like to shake you
up a little, even slap
your sagging face, to help you
say this final thing, to leap
the hurdle of the tumor and
the drugs and the lack of water
in your vessels, so you'll speak
this hanging truth, and make
your son, at least, more comfortable.

Orality

I try to get the world in my mouth,
expanding on the earlier work
with bottles and thumbs. I succeed
in my way, helping to break things
down. I can taste the preserving
salt in what's lived, the longing in smoke,
the froth of the vacuous.... I can give
my children forehead kisses and lift
their trepidations in through these lips.
I can take small parts of a woman
between my teeth to my tongue—for a few
breaths a certain tension is gone.
I can sip the pearls of my dying
father's dread from his cheek.

Woods I Never Entered

Rough ground, stony, root-ridged—
I remember, the shopping center
went up later. Woolworth's, Lord
& Taylor, Clem's barber shop
behind Florsheim Shoes—

I'm dreaming, while my father dies,
I'm walking between the oaks
and sycamores, where the Penn Fruit,
the record store I haunted for its
45s, the drugstore and its racy

magazines, replaced the woods
I never did explore before
they fell to these. Dreaming
a pathless swath, thick with vines—
like the golf course margins behind

Elliott's house, where my brother and I
slid down to the cliff-bottom
creek to search for salamanders.
Dad was not going to come
on such missions with his kids,

nor take us tromping through those woods.
Why do I go back to a tract
of lost forest where I never walked
while his chest decides the worth
of hauling the next breath?

It's as if I'd meet him there
were I to bushwhack in. I'd find
the kid he was, who must've stomped home

mud-covered from Cobbs Creek
once or twice before he grew up,

married Mom, and worked
his life away. He might still look
for me, for us, in there, the woods
I never entered, where now
and then we'd have dinner at Horn & Hardart's.

Before It Disappeared

He sinks away, less himself
and more a swollen sessile mass
planted in its hospice bed,

his eyes' whites like pond ice,
his lips unlicked and cracked,
his teeth in gluey jackets,

voice a scratchy aftermath
of what he meant to say and can't,
each breath his chest's next

fight with gravity—it asks
the question. The question springs
itself, up from the lumpen flesh,

the sinking country of his body,
and with all this history
in evidence, we, who lean

against the rails in reverence,
we cannot pose the question
properly. The fox who watched us

as we walked the creek-side trail
through the woods behind
the hospital just yesterday

held the question out to us
as well, before it disappeared
into the silence of the brush.

Two

Since

Loyal

Stacks of bills on the marble
dining room table, unopened cards
and letters (*sympathy* and still
some *get well*) scattered over
the kitchen counter, lists
on lined paper of accounts
where funds are held tucked under
long term care brochures
and prescription pill bottles,
the upstairs closets filled
with garments of no use here now,
cards with attorneys' numbers
on both bedroom dressers,
the nightstands' and the bathroom
drawers stuffed with the reminders
of obsolete necessities, slips
of colored memo pads still sticking
everywhere, and all the pictures,
books, clocks, boxes, curios...
the furniture of course, rugs
and tapestries, the curtains
shading no one from the glare
of the world, the house itself,
the ground it sits on still
requiring care—it comes down
to hair gel tubes, paperclips, scissors,
the little bronze French officer
under which lies the grocery list,
the almost-empty jar of marmalade
on the bottom shelf in the fridge,
and the dozens of frozen foil-wrapped
restaurant leftovers that would wait
forever if we let them. Things can be
loyal, more loyal than we are,
holding still, even for the dead.

First Days

We were herded back to our cars
after a few of us had spaded
some dirt onto the coffin's lid,

the polished box still
on that steel rack, suspended
over the hole. I missed

any mechanism by which it might
later be lowered—I've imagined
cranks, ropes, or something

akin to a forklift. Knowing
where he was going was meant
to be enough. To tell you

the truth, I'm finding it
hard to envision his cold flesh
in that plush compartment, let alone

under grass grown thick as the rest
around all the cut stones. Not such
a surprise, then, that I've glimpsed

that smile of his since—
off to my left and above
the shoulders of consoling guests.

Snippet

His illness stretched time
around him—the hours after
the surgery, in that white room
where we leaned close to listen
to lips quivering around whispers

he couldn't finish, the minutes
mud-thick valleys we couldn't cross,
his sinking into silence,
beginnings of thoughts coming
to no end. Food was placed

before him—he'd lost
all sense of sequence. Dinner? Lunch?
The fork seemed to hover
forever near his mouth, its morsel
of life cooling off. Days

somehow progressed, protracted
sunsets leached through the shades,
till they shipped him to the next
epoch—the rehab phase,
still in exile from his bed.

Then the era of the beams,
held still each day, ages
till the end of radiation. Then
months checking for what vigor might,
like new vegetation, extend

into the burn's devastation.
We watched him trudge the ramp's
switchbacks, walker against him,

toward the tavern entrance his last
Thanksgiving, refusing a hand.

The menu's print must've drifted
like uprooted kelp in surf,
the waitress's patience thinned
and deepened by turns.... Time,
a fluidic thing. His final

spring, he migrated
vast distances, sojourns
in cities he'd visit by train. We'd wait
in the pale blue hospice station
for his blinking return.

More and more, he'd squirm,
limbs in the thick of his weakness—
nameless pain, frame by frame.
We wished for him, for us,
a stillness.

Then it came—

now, his illness a snippet, fray
at the end of a ribbon of years,
like the mouth of a river, wind
and tide rip lifting a spray,
the air riddled with jewels.

Little Mr. Memory

Those nights I first called him Dad
when he found me awake in bed,
he'd beam to my Gettysburg Address,
to hear how I'd nearly memorized
the Periodic Table, or could recall
the names of the 1958 Men's
Finalists at Wimbledon. If I listed
the planets in order of distance from the sun,
then in order of mass, he'd laugh,
stunned. I was his Little Mr.
Memory. All I required was
that brilliant smile of his delivering
the chocolatiest chocolate milk
in West Philly, specially to me,
cup filled to the top and bubbly
from his spirited stir.

I didn't need the truth of the trouble—
we were agreed. Better the wonders
Pythagoras had discovered. Right
triangles, squares and square roots.
And the history of the future I would be
part of. America landing
on Mars, and here, the cure
for mortality, the antigravity
cars.... I told him I'd seen
the first great synthetic asteroid
colony orbiting the sun
on the cover of *Popular Science.*

It never went long. I'd guzzle
that marvelous darkened milk. Still,
before we were done, I'd run the names

of the noble gases, the forms
of cloud from cirrus to cumulonimbus
and what forms them, the arm's bones
and its purchase in the glenoid fossa,
the number of neutrons in both
the important uranium isotopes
and which was for fission—whatever might
hold him past the last sip. Some
nights he'd make it home for these minutes,
then he'd kiss my forehead, lift
the cup from my hands, and leave

the door open that one crucial inch,
permitting enough light in to remind me
I lived in the same world as Dad, who'd walk
down the stairs and into the argument
to which he did not know I'd listen,
and so he would not imagine
Little Mr. Memory still pondering
the mystery in the kitchen—two human
voices like waves in collision, the sharpness
and pitch carrying through that precision
gap in the doorway, through decades
and death, past cascades of birth—
echoing on in the lightless gel
of a busy man's brain as he tells
his brilliant little one our distance
from the sun is 93 million miles,
and there are 2.54 centimeters
to every inch.

His Ache in My Legs

A restless old man tried to rise again
from a railed bed in a strange place.
He did not understand where he was.
He'd lost interest in food and drink,
preoccupied with the train he knew
he needed to catch. His breath, at last,
an exasperated engine's chuff, gave
out. His chest had had enough—
all the tiny bellows caved. I had already
left. Then his eyes went out
and into their coves in his head.

Now after his name we say dead.
But I wake with his ache in my legs.
He never gave me the directions
to get to the station. I wander
the beds, poke into the shade
in the broken-down sheds, and wonder
if I'd stood by him more of my days,
his days, his hand on my shoulder,
sauntered side by side with him under
the vaulted beams of his belief
in the world, would we have arrived

on the platform, he in his gabardine
jacket, I in my brimmed felt hat,
on our way at last to the meeting
where the souls of the lost and the living
settle the score? A clay house,
between the last stop and the river,
where Isaac and Ishmael play
on the floor while the old men smoke
and drink dark tea—if I had stayed
longer, helped him rise to his feet
once more, would we have made it?

Up and Down

In the way a very small son can, I fell
up, after my first few footfalls
across the living room rug—up,

into the arms of the miraculous man
my father, before I can remember.
I kept falling up, out of the deep

admiration none of the blows undid—
when he seized the adolescent by the collar
after heaving open my locked bedroom door

and dragging me back down the stairs
where he tore my black beads of defiance
from my throat, I admired him more.

When I saw he could not stop driving
the ox of his body yoked to the broken-down
cart of his stubborn ambition, I wanted

to be more like him. When I listened
to the stutter coming out of the bald
irradiated head saying *Th-this is the best dinner*

ever, after he'd fought his walker
up through the tavern door insisting
he's getting better, I kept falling

harder, up into the thin air
of his mad optimism. Now, after
his heart's stopped, the beast's

remains under fresh dirt where I saw
the coffin slatted on its metal rack
over darkness, my animal form seeks

to fall toward his flesh, down, the pull
so strong I don't know how I've walked this level
ground, lugging my weight

through the days' dense light. Somewhere
around or above me—without arms
to catch me whether I fall up or down,

nor his mouth to sing one more song,
nor eyes to see his son's eyes cast down
on the earth his bones have entered—there

must be some high resonance, his
fool persistence a pure harmonic
refusing to disperse. This music,

beyond the range of these ears,
could it ripple the light? I'm looking
down, and can't see the shimmer.

My Body Decides

I knew his body, boxed
in oak, to be buried
in the Jewish cemetery
by Darby Creek. That day

we gathered, I laid
my eyes upon that casket
ready on its metal rack,
and, heavy, walked away.

The ache of it stayed
in my thighs, a weight
greater than gravity. Now,
later, come the sighs

out of my chest. My body
decides he's in the sky,
and the weightless part of me
tries to rise, to reach

the part of him that didn't die.

My Son Sees Something

My firstborn son must see my death wish
when I don't.
                                    Is it the flicker
of ghost looking out through my pupils
when I say goodnight? He looks right at me
and says, Why don't you walk to work
tomorrow, Dad? Or he watches as I watch
what's in the distance that isn't yet,
out past the flesh of his face and the rest
of the present. He hears the blessings
I sing in my chest to his unborn kids
at their weddings. He knows I attend
to breakfasts and bedtimes in houses
no one's built yet. I must be speaking,
deep in my breath, between the things
I mean to say, to him as to no other
being.
            For all the life force
still thrusting up out of me, frothing,
crashing into the world (what wrecked
that popsicle-stick raft of a marriage
I had with his mother), I must be scrawling
a message over and over in secret
from even myself, on the pages of air—
my heart's distraction with what happens after,
and he reads it, like a series of letters
delivered by homing pigeons who know
his devotion as home. For all the poems
of life I write, he reads the wonder
of later I must leave enclosed in the o
of love, the little dome of the e
in ever, the awninged shelter of a
in last.

It's not at all
that I want to be over. I'm beaming
with punky excitement for the next oyster
dinner, turned on by the woman
I catch turning her eyes from my face
when I face her across the tavern, jazzed
by imaginings of this summer's journey
along the shores of Alaska. But
I am becoming the past. It won't be
long—I'll lose the nest of these bones
as even a perch to watch from (let alone
touch).

My son sees me turning
a little translucent,

and someone reaching
out through the old man's skin, as if
to feel for a seam, a latch, a passage
to where my own father's gone,

where
everything can be seen at once.

She Told Me the Dream

Old man across the river—I mean
echo, apparition, wind
in the ferns and juniper—whether you listen
or not,
          I'm saying to you,
in that down-in-the-throat whisper
that goes everywhere, where you are
and are no longer my father, you can see,
just borrow my eyes it's alright
you gave them to me,
                              your son's
daughter whispering in Spanish
alone in the room where she packs to leave
for Buenos Aires,
                         the tattoo
you wouldn't approve of on her forearm
spelling *peace*.
                    Can you see
the confluence in her of two languages,
the breathing of one spirit
in two distant tribes,
                              the prospects
her breaths breed? What I imagine is
you're weeping with me, old resident
shimmer, old resonance
Father, sure you can borrow my heart
for this joy.
               She is all
the humble glory you'll need to have lived for,
folding her T-shirts and jeans
to fit in the carry-on,
                              holding
her fear and her hope in the same warm wrap

like the meat and vegetables she'll accept
in their flatbread envelope,

thanking

a friend, the air, the fields and slopes,
the possible everywhere, where you are,
where you found in the moment the freedom
to visit her in some kind of leap
as you left your body by the light
of one dawn last year.

She told me

the dream. Said you seemed at peace,
beaming, your hand on her shoulder.

My Grandmother's Demons

Dad said she was born in Russia,
a shtetl near St. Petersburg.
She swore she'd been born here,
Philadelphia. An American girl.

She was maybe four when they crossed—
crowded ship, ragged coats.
I'd never hear her tell it—the Cossacks,
their swords, torches.... She'd insist

she couldn't have seen it, bring out the borscht,
the brisket and tsimis, and beseech us
in Yiddish to eat, to eat more....
God, her need to be sure

we'd had enough. It was winter
and she listened as the wind blew in
its curses, killer flu, invisible
polio, the dark's dybbuks

who saw every emptiness as a nest—
she'd fill us like she filled her son, lest
the demons do, even here in the West,
where the murderers all speak English.

Wingtip Shoes

Visiting, weeks after the funeral,
I'm asked in on the business
of going through his things.

His shirts would billow around me,
pants cover my feet, my hands
never make it through his coat sleeves.

Some pairs of socks, I see, will fit.
Handkerchiefs, no problem, snug
in my hip pocket as in his.

Neckties—he'd sent me dozens
over dozens of years. They'd hang
past my belt, so they hang in my closet.

And those fine silk pocket squares
he'd tuck so deftly over his heart—
to what restaurant would I wear one?

There's a pair of brown wingtip shoes
I find in the attic. They look new.
Must've been a bit small for him

and the others who've had a look.
Laced up snug, they rise
with my heels off the rug. I'll wear them

sometimes. Out for dinner,
jacket, no tie, offering
to buy, like he did.

Blue

I'm watching the waves, from a beach
my father wouldn't have visited had he lived
hundreds of years. We've trespassed
on foot down a road that becomes a path
along this coast of igneous rock
on Kauai. I watch the crests rise
and thin, till they begin to bend
toward the shore, at which moment they lens
the sky instead of the deeper water
and turn from green to a crystalline blue,
till they arc down further and whiten
in the churn of their return to the body
they rise from. What my father knew
was the future, what would become, the man
I would be. What he never saw,
with all his days on the beach as a kid
and more with his own kids later, is what
I'm watching, wishing my eyes were his
and he could at last come to see this
luminous blueness through the ridges
of tide the wind and moon lift up
from the green world of unconsciousness. This—
the blue of innocence before chaos, blue
of the newborn's eyes before pigments arise,
blue of a sky that possesses nothing
itself but allows the higher energy
radiance of the blue light free passage,
blue that my father would sing was *smilin'*
at me, though I'm somehow sure
he never really peered into the empty
miracle of blue, vast banner of pure
possibility—it's what I saw when he lifted me
up from the white froth rushing in

right at my face, and I floated
weightless a moment, at the height
of his strong gentle toss of my slight mass
just inches aloft from the hands I knew
would catch me by the chest, I little sheaf
of his unspoken wishes, as we watched
the waves rise, reaching it seemed,
for that bright blue world of belief.

Tiny Mirrors

The kid taught himself. He'd have to
hurl that Duncan, fast off his hand,
string slot perfectly vertical, down
to a half-inch off the pavement, watch it
spin in frictionless sleep, time
slowed down by the magic, give it
that tweak of the wrist to snap it
back up the twine, obedient
fat little disc at home in his palm—
walking the dog, around the world,
cat's cradle—he'd get it,
watching the older kids on the street
and repeating, repeating, in private,
back of the house on the concrete
walkway between the tomato vine rows.
He'd beat those big kids in a week.

And the best batters' stances, he'd watch—
eyes teaching shoulders, arms, hips,
he'd fathom the multiple arcs
of the swings that could hurtle the ball
out of the schoolyard. He'd practice
back in the alley till dark. Homework
finished, set for the next day's
A on the math test, he'd catch the game
at Connie Mack on the radio, then dream
the Goodman aria he'd master,
the clarinet's sleek black and silver
light in the cradle of his fingers
before the rapt crowd in the school
auditorium, wake to the outfit laid out,
necktie, cufflinks, white collar's studs,
worsted cuffed wool slacks, wingtips

and all—he'd be the man
who'd swing the most adorable girl
away from his graceful embrace and back
to the wows of the attracted circle
on the gym floor, the Dorsey number
echoing against the walls and washing
across the faces of those gathered
gawky admirers. He'd be buoyed
on such tide all his days. In the pool halls
he'd lean with learned poise into shots
that called for the side-spin he'd got down
the late hours he'd found to repeat
and repeat, till it came without thought.
Looked like a natural. At watching
and working the know-how into his tissue,
he was. Driven to work at it—

tennis lifted him out of West Philly
and onto the varsity team at Penn,
Cuban music and mambo moved him
into the Atlantic City hotels
to win the dance contests, to win the woman
he'd marry, and at work selling homes,
over the shoulders of the architects,
he'd find his way into the blueprints,
mapping out island kitchens that sold
the units in the developments.
In the necktie business, he'd learn
the islands where the wool was shorn,
reach inside the machines in the mills
in England, count by the feel in his fingers
the densities of the weaves of the silk
in the Italian factories. He'd watch

and listen, repeat and repeat,
allowing all that thrilled him inside
to become the twine of his sinews,
seeming to his kids to have known it
always. Driven to have known it,
to the point of having forgotten
how it had come to him. The time—
I can't imagine where he'd found it.
They say in our brains there are mirror
neurons by which we reflect
down into these motors our bodies
whatever enters our eyes we are moved
to emulate. I see him watching
a lanky hero at a clay court baseline
bringing the racket up and around
from behind over his head and down

with a stifled grunt, the ball flying
just over the net, the man running
to meet the return shot. I see the kid
who would be my father clenching
his already broad left hand
on the leather of his dream-racket, teaching
his muscles the form and the force
for the first real match, repeating
the sequence into the night, no one,
not even himself, knowing how much
practice he's putting into it. Driven
inside where those tiny mirrors tilt
like sails catching the world's light,
he's working the tide that will carry him
all the years of his life, already
admired in the quiet of the afterworld.

This One Leaf

Under the dawn's ripe-apricot sky,
  I and the rest of the living return
to our limbs, lungs, watery eyes,

in through our mouths and nostrils, in
  through our pierceable skins, from our other
lives and battles, other skies.

Under December's silvered rooftops,
  we rise. Under the wall
of the hillside's green-black trees, we begin

to remember our lives, forgetting
  the dead we survive, leaving the angels
who'd lighted our dreams alone again, turning

from the ghosts with whom we'd taken up
  griefs and hopes unspoken by daylight.
Waking we call it. Back in the spin

of electron and planet, friction
  and press of the blood's pulse, heave
of the breath, hoist and trudge of the flesh

down the hall, face in the glass—is this
  the actual? I want to keep this
one russet leaf I've torn off, brought

back from the beech grove where I stood
  with my father a minute ago, ankle-deep
in the mud, agreeing we'll find the road.

The Ghost in His Chest

He's come down from the trees, up
from the earth—in, through the breath,
to sit with me in the hearth of my chest,
and I'm pleased. To hell with his death—

we converse. I need move no lips.
And were I deaf, I'd catch every word
he emits. Now that he lives by my nerves,
now that his formulations follow

my cerebral tissue's twists, now
that I can at last get him tipsy on sips
of the whiskey he'd never touch, he comes
to know who his son is. I tell him

things I couldn't face to face.
What a mess he made of his marriage.
How he pursed his lips and looked
into the distance to distance himself

when anyone placed an issue too tough
on the table beside the sliced tomatoes,
bagels, and lox. Now he says yes,
he was an ass, wishes he'd listened

in the flesh. I'll take his confession,
silent, unwritten, and raise my glass
for us both, an aging man and the ghost
in his chest. It doesn't get better than this.

Study in Red

I'm working from memory. My children's
births—those first moments in light,
umbilical conduit open, both worlds
inherited at once, the legacy of blood
(from before it ever ran red) and the blind
objecthood of every thing from the body
to death's bed. What did I impart?

From memory, it's said. My brother
and I inherited the territory of our mother's
and father's dreads (those silent currents
of something like blood but not red) pulsing
wordless and imageless at our temples,
carving the valleys ahead. How many
lives to arrive at forgiveness (religious

question we atheists kept as a secret
from ourselves)? And what was the difference?
Jacob and Esau, Wally and the Beaver....
We were the cartoon warriors from space,
matinee saviors of an undeserving race
of mothers and fathers. And what of Aunt Dorothy,
our grandparents? Screaming intruders,

fondlers, poking the past into us
with their blame-fat fingers, stuffing us
on chicken and mashed potatoes (as if
we were starving in our mother's care). We were
heirs to the murderous fuss of the nomad
scramble, every meal a suspense
as if the table were pressed to the rail

on a thronged deck, the gale ready to toss us
(as if we were still on the long crossing
to that America where brothers inherit
no dread, no blame, no guilt, no sunset
red as the blood of pogroms). I'm working
from memory. I am sorry I left
my brother to look after our bitter mother.

Sure of What's Needed

My brother's period sticks to the air
after whatever he says. Hello.
It won't be possible to meet then. Take care.

Is it the same tiny bottomless blackness
he plants again at the end of each utterance,
or one of a weightless infinity
from his invisible satchel? No one asks

how he supplies himself with so many
seeds of finality. I imagine
they're not hard to harvest. I see them
sometimes, floating in close, between us

in parks and bars. In train stations.
Don't worry, says my optometrist.
Mine, anyway, are just twisted commas.

It's the little solo dot of darkness,
a singularity, absolute, that
my brother drills instantly into the atmosphere
endlessly ending a permanent sentence.

That's what I fear. It won't budge
under any pressure, can't be cajoled
or nudged. Never seduced by love
or anger. It will not disappear.

Maybe it's nailed right into the matrix
that upholds all appearances forever.
Maybe he manufactures millions
of these impervious infinitesimal pellets

in his ultra-tidy apartment. Can he sew them
like buttons to close the lips of those
who would kiss him? Does he keep himself

snapped into the suit of his skin with them,
dry in a full-body splashguard against
the slobbering tide of the world? I can't
ask him. But I can wonder

what spoons flew through his lips' least parting,
what tremulous palms pressed at his neck, whose
voices in ceaseless counterpoint penetrated
his half-sleep from the live opera downstairs.

I can see how a hard point of nothingness might
stop a needle in flight, without
the needler knowing. That would be perfect.

I could've used a device like that too,
but I batted and yelled. I was crude.
I held my own, and left soon.

My brother appears to have cooperated—
he's helped the folks all these years, down
to hospital statements, snow shovels, light bulbs,

and funeral arrangements. Always on hand,
sure of what's needed, he stands
in the kitchen, and from some inner distance,

he listens, takes notes even,
and without quite looking at anyone,
provides his opinion. A plan. Period.

Watching the Perseids

The broadcast's breaking up in static—
solar flares, snow, ozone
fluctuations, I don't know.

Should I care? I can still play the message
my phone captured one year back—
"*No Time for Love*"—he sings

the refrain in that same boyish tone
I'd heard come out of him over a steak,
or climbing the bleachers to our seats,

my hand in his, before
a night game at Connie Mack. Even
on his way out in the cold in the dawn

to catch the train, singing whatever
he said—his brisk See ya *lat*-er!
down the steps. See ya to-*night*!

Singing the tireless dance of his life—
he left no time in it for the quiet
closeness of watching the Perseids

or the river from its banks, the fire's
sparks disappearing into the dark....
Not until it was near the time

for hospice, to never again know
where he was. Those last hours on his own
bed, I'd lie beside him and we'd sing

whatever old tune came into either
one of our heads. Quiet.
Like watching the tide.

Now, his music is drowning
in surf-sound. My brain's magic
receiver is shorting out. Or is it

the train I hear, him on it, still
singing, voice going remote
in the clatter and hiss? Has he lifted

the ticket out of his coat pocket,
handed it over to the conductor,
and sat back, softly sounding out

Lullaby of Birdland? I can wonder,
try to hear his voice in the white noise
between my ears, while he travels

like the seasoned commuter he was
to that city past the meteors, out
past the planets, in the stars.

Sure

You spoke from experience, you said,
one hand on the wheel, one arm free
to catch the sun and the rush of air
by the Buick's rolled-down window. How,
sitting there, steering us through
the quiet intersection by the grammar school,
you seemed to field my tears and sputters
like pop flies easy to get under
well before they landed, welcoming
my trouble with Mom's temper, struggle
with my own, the tension I knew
as a rope in my innards twisted by all
the hatreds (Mom's for you, your mother's
needles through every soul, your sister's
drunken curses…), my little brother's
sickness with stealing telephones
from local businesses on weekends,
the nightly damage to your marriage, none of it
more than the breeze in your forearm's hairs
as you steered and seemed to listen, all of it
nothing to worry about—how I envied
the sureness of your speech, your lips
together in peace as you formed each thought,
your voice like the lap of slack tide in a harbor,
telling us both, nothing's too rough
in this life. Sure. How you practiced
the positive, like a mercury atom,
nucleus independent and claiming
no wicked little electrons, shadowless
cloud a kid colors in with white wax,
sailing over a house on the ground
with no ground behind it, only the blue
of sky blue sky around it. How

existence allowed you this impossibility
I already knew was a mystery
when I was six. I didn't see you
desperate until I was sixty—then
you flailed against the steel-rail stasis
of the hospice bed, your terminal inertia
intolerable—what you'd never experienced
as long as you'd cruised ahead, steadily
through the rages around you. Finally,
an intersection you couldn't glide through,
a ball you couldn't catch without crashing
into the wall. No more at the wheel,
all the sureness went out of your voice,
your lips hung apart, you couldn't finish
a thought, and I assured you (my hand
on the brow of the head you could no longer lift
to look forward) you'd done it all, nothing
rough on the road before you, just shadow
and stillness. I was sure, I said.

Far from His Bed

Dolomite Point, New Zealand

A year ago, I wouldn't have traveled
anywhere but to my father's bed.
We'd already had our last times
out in the car, to get lunch,
or to stop by Jimmy's for a trim
as if everything was alright. He was
pretty much upstairs for good by then,
until he got shipped out for good
when he got too difficult. A year ago
he still wanted to go places he couldn't,
and he couldn't quit this.

He got more
delirious. There was a train station
some of the time in the bedroom mirror.
The best thing for it was a hand
stroking his forehead, and some words
about how we could just be together
here, him in his bed. And the old
songs we could sing. He sang them
better than most even then, unable
to finish a spoken sentence.

A year ago, he hadn't reckoned
that he wouldn't be getting back out
on the road. It would never be
his intention to forsake his own flesh
to set himself free. Nonetheless,
on his body's insistence a few months later,
he left. And freed us to wander
as far from his bed as we'd ever gone,
and I did, with his songs in my head.

The Earth's Business

A year in the ground, so we drove there
to stand before the engraved stone.

As we came onto the cemetery road,
a fat gopher ran across the cracked asphalt.

No one else was there. It was clear,
and the air still. We were slow

on the stretch of paved path from the car,
till we reached his marker, and stood there,

his wife steadied between his two sons,
in the shade of the tree they'd planted him under,

good a place as any in this quiet
city of loved ones' remains,

where what goes on is the earth's business,
except for the visitors' comings and goings.

But wasn't he home in bed, or downtown
at his desk? Aren't we going to meet him

at that restaurant, the one with the great shrimp
cocktail and those fine cuts of steak?

Aren't we here in the shade by mistake?
Well, we hadn't quite visited yet.

As we walked across the bare lot to the car,
in the sun, in the silence, winding

before us, a thin white-striped snake.

Coda

This is my candle for you Father.
A small synaptic fire.

This the stone I place where you rest.
One of the bones of my wrist,

still in its flesh, pressed
to the wooden earth of my desk.

My prayer for you, curling out
from my mouth, between atoms of air.

And this is my letter. Dear Father,
The farther you drift, the nearer.

Jed Myers is also the author of *The Nameless* (Finishing Line Press, 2014). He won the 2012 Mary C. Mohr Editors' Award offered by *Southern Indiana Review*, and received the 2013 *Literal Latte* Poetry Award. His poems have appeared in *Prairie Schooner, Nimrod International Journal, Crab Orchard Review, Atlanta Review, Crab Creek Review*, and elsewhere.

Myers grew up in Philadelphia. He studied poetry at Tufts University, then studied medicine, and migrated to Seattle, where he's raised three children and is a psychiatrist with a therapy practice. The events of September 11, 2001 compelled him to engage more fully in the arts. A musician as well, he seeks ways to bring poetry and music together, and hosts the long-running open-mic cabaret NorthEndForum in Seattle's Ravenna neighborhood.